Michael's Picture

Written and Illustrated by
Michael Grejniec

Celebration Press
*An Imprint of Addison-Wesley
Educational Publishers, Inc.*

I can make a hippopotamus.

I can make a tiger.

I can make a zebra.

I can make a bird.

I can make a rabbit.

I can make a turtle.

Here's my picture!